How to
Ruin
Your Life

Other Hay House Titles
of Related Interest

Books

*How to Get from Where You Are to Where
You Want to Be,* by Cheri Huber

Simple Things, by Jim Brickman,
with Cindy Pearlman

Weight Loss for the Mind, by Stuart Wilde

Audio Programs

Dr. Phil Getting Real, by Dr. Phil McGraw

*How to Get What You Really, Really, Really,
Really Want,* by Dr. Wayne W. Dyer
and Deepak Chopra, M.D.

How to Overcome Life's Problems,
by Joan Borysenko, Ph.D.

Card Decks

If Life Is a Game, These Are the Rules
(a 50-card deck), by Chérie Carter-Scott, Ph.D.

Until Today (a 50-card deck), by Iyanla Vanzant

❁ ❁ ❁

All of the above are available at your local bookstore,
or may be ordered through Hay House, Inc.:

(800) 654-5126 or **(760) 431-7695**
(800) 650-5115 (fax) or **(760) 431-6948 (fax)**
www.hayhouse.com

How to
Ruin
Your Life

Ben Stein

Hay House, Inc.
Carlsbad, California • Sydney, Australia
Canada • Hong Kong • United Kingdom

Published and distributed in the United States by: Hay House, Inc.,
P.O. Box 5100, Carlsbad, CA 92018-5100 • (800) 654-5126 • (800) 650-5115
(fax) • www.hayhouse.com • *Published and distributed in Australia
by:* Hay House Australia Pty Ltd, P.O. Box 515, Brighton-Le-Sands, NSW
2216 • *phone:* 1800 023 516 • *e-mail:* info@hayhouse.com.au • *Distributed
in the United Kingdom by:* Airlift, 8 The Arena, Mollison Ave., Enfield,
Middlesex, United Kingdom EN3 7NL • *Distributed in Canada by:*
Raincoast, 9050 Shaughnessy St., Vancouver, B.C., Canada V6P 6E5

Editorial supervision: Jill Kramer • *Design:* Jenn Ramsey

Library of Congress Cataloging-in-Publication Data

Stein, Ben.
    How to ruin your life / Ben Stein.
        p. cm.
    ISBN 1-56170-974-3
    1. Conduct of life—Humor. I. Title.
    BJ1595 .S76 2002
    158.1'02'07—dc21

                             2002000760

ISBN 1-4019-974-3

05 04 03 02   4 3 2 1
1st printing, September 2002

Printed in the United States of America

❖ ❖ ❖

For Alex, my wifey,
who has often saved me
from ruining my life;
for our son, Tommy,
whom I love to pieces;
and for all good dogs and cats.

❖ ❖ ❖

CONTENTS

ACKNOWLEDGMENTS

For all of the people whose terrible examples showed me the paths to avoid and made writing this book a snap; and for my father and mother; my wife, Alex; my best friend, Al Burton; my dear, indispensable pals Phil DeMuth, Paul Hyman, Dr. Garth Wood (may he rest in peace), Sid Dauman, Wlady Pleszcynzski, John Coyne, Aram Bakshian, Julie and David Eisenhower, Larry Lissitzyn, Arthur Best, Susan Sgarlat, Bob Tyrrell, Marcia Hurwitz, Norman Lear, Andrew Golder, Debbie Liebling, Jimmy Kimmel, Meredith Fox, Sal Iacono, Yaniv Malka, and Susie Pannenbacker, and others who showed me how to get off the road to disaster not once but many times; and especially for the men and women of the nooner in Point Dume, Malibu; and finally, for Pat Davis, who taught me how to live in the moment.

INTRODUCTION

Why Failure Matters

"Success," said John F. Kennedy, "has a hundred fathers. Failure is an orphan." I think he said it about the failed invasion of Cuba at The Bay of Pigs in 1961, but it certainly applies to "how to" books and articles as well. In any bookstore, there will be dozens of titles on how to succeed, many with the same advice, just a different typeface.

It's fairly obvious to any shopper that there aren't many books or articles on how to fail. Yet, as any parent knows, you can learn just as much by studying the people who fail as the people who succeed. In fact, failure is often a virtual road map to success—in reverse. Trace the route to poverty, loneliness, obscurity, and despair . . . and then go in exactly the opposite direction . . . and you can wind up with comfort, good company, a fine reputation, and high self-confidence.

Moreover, it's been fascinating to me to observe that while successful folks have all kinds of different routes to triumph (some as simple as luck and inheritance), failures have a lot in common. Unhappy families who have lost out on the good things in life are all alike, as one might say, to alter a famous phrase by Tolstoy. If you can avoid the ways and means that losers take to wreck their lives, you may not necessarily get to be a huge success, but you'll certainly avoid failure—at least self-inflicted, dismal failure. If you can stay out of the heavy, obsessive gravity of self-destruction and its many tentacles, then you're well on your way to succeeding.

Now, you may ask why I'm qualified to write this book, and you should. Mainly it's because I am, by nature, a tourist everywhere I go, especially at home, and I spend much of my time and energy analyzing what I observe. I've been following failure intently since I was in elementary school (and maybe earlier). Charged by my overbearing but loving mother with not allowing myself to become a failure, I've tried to note what failures did in algebra class, in the gym, on dates, at work, at play—everywhere I've gone. Also, there are braver men and women than I am; better-looking ones; and smarter, stronger ones. But few have completed as many different projects and been involved in as many different fields as I have. As such, I've been privileged to observe failure in the Ivy League, in the field of law, in the world of finance, in the White House (and oh, what a failure!), in Hollywood circles, in the Academy—just about everywhere.

As noted, I observe a great deal of similarity in these failures and in what leads to failure. And this, my combination of experience and analytical practice, qualifies me to write this book—and might even encourage you to read it.

But in any event, let the advice given here speak for itself. If you don't find this material compelling, just put the book down and stop reading it. (This also will help you in your efforts to become a failure.)

Why, by the way, are there 35 steps? Well, why not? That's how many I came up with that related to broad categories (such as relationships, money, family, and so on). I could have included lesser categories such as "Pierce your nose," but that's another story. I could have included ones of genuine value such as "Wear brown when you're expected to wear gray or dark blue," but this also comes under other, larger categories.

If you haven't found enough ways to ruin your life by the time you come to the end of this book, you never needed it in the first place. You were just born knowing how to lose.

So, without further ado, offered to you with the sure knowledge that you won't see anything of yourself or anyone you know (yeah, right) in any of these tidbits, herewith is some guidance on "How to Ruin Your Life," and maybe on how not to.

Follow these rules and you're guaranteed disaster. Avoid them, and you're on the high road to achievement and success.

❀ ❀ ❀   ❀ ❀ ❀

1

Don't Learn Any Useful Skills

Make yourself useless. Don't practice decent study habits. Don't bother to acquaint yourself with history, languages, or mathematics. Don't develop any special advanced skills in law, architecture, medicine, or electrical contracting. When others sacrifice their fun times studying and attending classes, just laugh at them and stay in bed watching old movies. (In fact, a general attitude of ridiculing any genuine effort by yourself or others is also a major way to ruin your life, but more on that later.) As others learn to produce real value for the world by healing disease, making candles, applying makeup, cutting hair, or tracking inventory, don't bother to learn anything specialized or useful at all.

Yes, it's true that there's a mountain of experience and data that tell us that education and skills are the tickets to a secure, happy life. But none of that applies to *you*. Many say that others will have bigger, better lives if they acquire a skill, trade, or advanced degree. Again, none of that means a thing to you. You'll have all of the great things in life anyway. You're special, unique in every way. Just coast by on your wit and good looks. You're a wheeler and a dealer.

What kind of education did Rhett Butler have, after all? What kind did Elvis Presley have? I didn't see Madonna in grad school or P. Diddy (or whatever name he's going by these days) either. Yet look at how far they went. You'll do at least as well with good luck and fortune that just happen to drop into your lap. Make sure that you take as examples of how to ruin your life the one in a billion who succeeds *without* skills . . . instead of the 99 out of 100 who succeed *with* skills.

You were born knowing all you need to know, and don't you forget it. Avoid getting any education that smacks of the ordinary and the mundane. You're not ordinary. You're special, and I'll say it until you understand it. It's vital that you know that your uniqueness will get you through every crisis. You'll get by just by being *you*. Training is for the masses, not for classy folk like yourself. You're fated to be rich and famous, and you don't have to do one more thing to get it other than what you've already done. Just sit back and be your own uniquely great and lovable self.

❁ ❁ ❁

2

Don't Learn Any Self-Discipline

Be a slob. Hey, you're not at West Point or in boot camp! You're a chilled-out, mellowed-out dude. You deserve all of the rest you can get. You need your snooze time. You need to see that movie running on the inside of your eyelids. And don't feel guilty that you're under the covers while everyone else is out working. It's not your fault that they're nine-to-five losers. Just stay in the sack and get up whenever you feel like it. Once you do get up, stay up as long as you want. There are lots of great old films on TV. Plus, there are those fabulous reruns of *Married . . . with Children* and *The Simpsons*. Nothing you could do during the day could possibly be as fruitful as watching Bart shoot down Homer for the millionth time. I mean, that's great stuff, right? And you're a real night owl, so what's the point of hitting the sack before 3 A.M.?

And don't think about the morning, because you're not going to be up then, anyway. Morning is for farmers, and I don't think a cool dude like you is going out to be cleaning out the cow stalls. Am I right?

Eat anything you want, too. Hey, you look great no matter how much you weigh. You were just born gorgeous. If you're a few hundred pounds more than those twigs in the fashion magazines, that's their problem. They're anorexic. Anyway, you have a lot on your mind, and it feels soothing to eat. So eat whatever you want whenever you want. That's your right! This country is a miracle of agricultural production, and it would be insulting to our ranchers to snub their steak and cheese and milkshakes. Plus, when you have nothing better to do, why not mosey on over to the fridge and have a bite? I mean, who's looking? You're not in a freaking police state, are you? Just eat that leftover cake or apple pie and be done with it.

Now, this part is really important: *Don't make yourself work when you'd rather play.* In fact, don't work at all if you don't feel like it. Life is short. Why should you spend even one second of it doing a darned thing you don't want to do? Hey, maybe they didn't hear, but there's a 13th Amendment to the Constitution abolishing slavery! If you did have to work, then why did they bother to fight the Civil War? What was the point of Lincoln getting assassinated if you have to sweat and toil? Forget it. You don't have to do anything you don't want to do. You're better than that. In fact, you're better than anyone or anything else on earth. You have the right to refuse to do any work you don't feel like doing. Somehow the money will come to you simply because you want it to, whether you work or not.

Don't bother to develop any sense of discipline in anything and you'll be really happy and proud of yourself! You're a big cuddly baby, and everyone will always adore you for it, even when you're a graying, paunchy, middle-aged fella.

❀ ❀ ❀

3

※ ※ ※ ※ ※ ※

Convince Yourself You're the Center of the Universe

Face it: You're the only one who matters in any given situation. The truth is—and let me be the first to tell you—God went away on vacation and left you in charge! Why bother taking into account that your wife wants you to clean out the garage? Why should you even listen when your husband tells you he'd like to have a home-cooked meal for the first time in a year? So what if your parents say you haven't done any chores around the house in a month? Who gives a darn if your roommate tells you that your socks are so dirty that the smell is keeping him up at night? *Who cares?* You're the only one who counts!

Why listen to anyone else's troubles? Your problems are the ones that make the difference. If someone else's parent is sick, hey, that's their deal. If the guy who helped you with your math exam now wants you to help him wash his truck, too darned bad for that loser. Just walk right on by, but *do* expect other people to listen to you and do what you want when you want it.

So what if, after a while, no one wants to talk to you? That's just proof of what dirtbags they are. By the way, does a living, breathing deity need to have anyone to converse with? I don't think so, do you? Where *you* want to eat, where *you* want to go on vacation, where *you* want to live—that's all that matters. The whole world has got to get it straight. You come first, and there won't be any peace anywhere until everybody sure as hell knows it.

Look at it this way. Imagine that Moses came back to earth with a special 11th Commandment, and that commandment is that you're the boss for the next hundred years. Then Moses shakes your hand and gives you his staff right on worldwide TV. That's how you have to believe your destiny was shaped. Act on it minute by minute.

❀ ❀ ❀

4

Never Accept Any Responsibility for Anything That Goes Wrong

Play the blame game. It's always someone else's fault, or else it's just bad luck. You failed your algebra class? You obviously had a lousy teacher. The other kids passed? They were brownnosers. The cops gave you a ticket because you were driving recklessly? Hey, you had a lot on your plate that day, *and* you had a late night before. You lost your job because you didn't show up on time for a week? Wow, who can work those kind of hours anyway?

Whatever it was, you didn't mean to do it wrong; anyhow, it's a hassle to have to hear someone bitching at you. (Did the pharaohs have to listen to anyone complaining about them? Did Allah? Or the Buddha? Then why should you?!) Basically, you have no responsibility for doing anything right, and if it doesn't go smoothly, that's someone else's problem. Your mom didn't raise you to get yelled at. There's a simple rule in this world: If it's bad, it's someone else's tough luck and you don't want to hear about it.

The world should know this by now: It's no fun to be criticized, and that means it's no fun for *you* to be criticized. You're free, indeed required, to insult and blame others. But as the official designee of the Almighty to be His Deputy on Earth, obviously you're above it all. That's clear, right? Okay, 'nuff said. You don't deserve to take the heat for anything—but everyone else does. (Oh, by the way, always claim credit for everything good, and deny everything bad . . . but you knew that already, didn't you?)

5

Criticize Early and Often

Always make sure to be the caustic critic. Let's face it: There isn't enough complaining in this world. There's too much Pollyanna-ish cheer and frivolity. Too many people just smile and let things go. Don't go along with them. There's something wrong with *every-thing and everyone* if you look closely enough, and by golly, you have to make it your job to find it first and complain about it loudest.

Let's take some easy examples: Your wife might look pretty good when she's setting out on her first day of work, but is every single, solitary hair in its place? Let her know that she doesn't look perfect enough. Don't let her get away with not looking her best. And maybe she's gained a bit of weight. Tell her that you've noticed those extra pounds. Make sure you point it all out. After all, you're just being constructive.

Your husband used up most of his Saturday mowing the lawn? Fine, but how about putting in some new plants to give the yard some color! Let him have it—why should he have any chance to relax? Get him out there working while you lounge in front of the TV. Your son did well in his last soccer game? Okay, but he missed two goals that looked easy to you. Why let him off the hook? Why let *anyone* off easy? Your daughter is doing great at gymnastics? Well, if she's so great, why didn't she get the gold medal at the last meet? She must have screwed up in some way. Let her know you that you've been paying attention, and criticize her until she sobs in frustration. That should make her do better next time.

What's the point of your being the world's most gifted observer and critic if you end up wasting all of your special talents and let people slide by?

Spare the criticism and you spoil the wife (or husband or child or employee or friend or whatever). The whole world needs to know that they're far from perfect. They can't just go about lollygagging and thinking they're doing fine. They need help—just as surely as you *don't* need it.

You're the important one, the perfect one, and people have to pay attention to what you say. The world is a crappy place anyway, right? Laying withering criticism on every situation assures that everyone knows you're in charge— and everyone is lucky that you are!

❦ ❦ ❦

6

❖ ❖ ❖ ❖ ❖ ❖

Never Be Grateful

And I mean never! Why should you? Think about it for a minute: You live in the richest, freest, most beautiful country in the world. Of course you have a great car and air conditioning and a comfortable place to live, but there's still lots to be angry about. I mean, isn't Bill Gates richer than you are? Isn't Ashley Judd better looking? Isn't Britney Spears more famous? Isn't Tiger Woods a better golfer? So why should you be grateful? You have a lot to be sore about.

True, a lot of sappy sentimentalists might be grateful for small favors, but you're a hard-headed realist. You can see that our whole society is going to hell in a handbasket.

Just a few examples will make the case easily: What's with music today? It's horrible, and is obviously rotting the brains of our young people. What about the obscene way teenagers dress? Yes, the kids may like it, but isn't it all really about how it affects *you?* And if *you* don't like it, what do you have to be grateful for? (And while we're at it, make sure you always think in this way: How does it affect *you?* Nothing else and no one else matters.) Remember that checkout clerk at the grocery store? Well, she practically ruined your morning with her sappy "Have a nice day." It's impossible to be grateful with such revolting behavior in your midst.

What about the environment? Yes, it might look okay where you are, but what about in the national forests out West? There's a drought, and fires galore! And right here at home, isn't your wife's cooking or your husband's woodworking lacking in the proficiency department? You bet. There's not much room for gratitude with suffering like this going on. There's plenty to moan about.

And please don't forget to feel ungrateful toward your parents. What did they ever do for you? Sure, they stayed up nights with you for years. Okay, maybe they got up early when they didn't want to so they could get you to school on time. And yes, they might have worked extra hours or even two jobs to get you the car or summer camp excursion you wanted. But that was what they *owed* you. You were their child. It should have been a pleasure and a gift to make sacrifices for you. Now, of course, you don't feel as if it's a pleasure and a gift to get up at six to get your own kid off to school. *But that's the exact point, friend! You are special and different, and people owe you in a way that you don't owe anyone else.*

So do yourself a big favor: Don't let gratitude even enter your mind. The world hasn't completely bowed down before your perfection yet, and it's very far from being a perfect place, so what's there to be grateful for? If you start feeling gratitude—even in some small way—that means you're weak, so forget it.

❧ ❧ ❧

7

Know That You're the Source of All Wisdom

The world needs your advice to run properly—not just your criticism, but your guidance. Have you noticed what a mess society is in? Horrifying terrorism at home and abroad. This wouldn't have happened if *you* had been running the FBI and the CIA, or if they'd at least called you every day for your words of wisdom. War in the Middle East? You could easily avert it if Messrs. Arafat and Sharon would just ask *you* what should be done in the Gaza Strip and Tel Aviv. Starvation in Africa? You have the solution right under your hat. But have the fools asked *you?* No, they did not. Crime in the streets? Serious spread of the AIDS virus? Religious rancor? Turmoil in the stock market and widespread financial fraud? Why? Because the world isn't getting enough of *your* advice! You know more than anyone else about finance, counterterrorism, peace among and within religions, and the control of infectious diseases.

Yes, I already mentioned criticism, but this is something different. This is about advice— not just saying "nay," but offering specific pointers. The world is in a mess because too much of its business goes on without anyone consulting you and getting your marching orders.

And it gets worse right within your circle. One friend is getting a divorce; another one is gaining weight. Still another one is losing his job and maybe his house. And one's kid can't get her schoolwork done. Why? Well, there are a lot of causes (mostly because if they ain't you, their name is *loser!*), but only one sure cure: Consult you and get *your* advice. You would most assuredly know how to solve every one of those dilemmas in a heartbeat.

Why don't they ask? Because they're jealous and not as smart as you are. But just because they don't ask, that doesn't mean you shouldn't offer your unsolicited advice. In fact, to be generous about it, you should positively insist that they heed your words of wisdom immediately, and take notes while they're at it. *You* know how to save that marriage. *You* know how to get that guy's job back, and you can certainly turn that kid into an A student.

And if your neighbors are too darned incompetent to ask, you have to get in their faces and make them know what's best for them. Don't let any minor blemishes in your own life slow you down for even one minute as far as putting in your two cents' worth is concerned. The point is that people have to learn to do as you say, not as you do. It's your duty as a god who walks the earth to make sure that everyone gets the benefit of your experience on every issue. Please don't forget it. And when you *do* give your advice, don't be stingy with it. Go into long-winded detail, and make sure they get it right by going over whatever you say over and over and over again.

✦ ✦ ✦

8

※ ※ ※ ※ ※ ※

Envy Everything;
Appreciate Nothing

Envy everyone. For example, your neighbor has a better lawn. Forget the possibility that this is because he worked harder tending it, watering it, and fertilizing it. Logic plays no part here. Just the fact that he has that emerald green lawn is reason enough for envy. The other neighbor has a Caddy while you have an old Yugo. Never mind that he worked long hours and got a second degree by going to school at night so he could get a better job. He's got a better car. That, by itself, is plenty reason to feel envy. Or how about the guy who hangs out next to you at the tavern? He just got a beautiful young girlfriend and you've been observing (and pointing out!) that your wife is getting a bit hippy. Never mind that your wife is the most loyal creature on this earth. Never mind her devotion and kindness to you over the decades. Just forget about that stuff. In fact, forget about everything in your life that's good. *Only concentrate on what you don't have that other people do.*

That mother's kid got into Harvard. So what if she worked with him for hours on his papers and extracurricular activities while you snoozed. The kid is still getting into Harvard, while yours will be lucky to graduate from high school. Plenty of reason to feel envy. Especially since, as we know, if somebody isn't you, he's a loser by definition.

That one's wife has a better figure than yours. Of course she's also always in a bad mood from dieting, and she never has a nice word to say, but she *does* have a good build, so there's reason to feel still more envy. That one's husband has a more lucrative job than yours. Hey, come to think of it, when you start, there's almost everything to envy and almost nada to be happy about. Just make your way down the road to envy and you won't ever return. You'll just get more and more envious until you disappear right up your own exhaust.

Envy is a perfect poison. Taken regularly throughout the day, it can ruin anything decent going on in your life. Therefore . . . don't forget to take it in good measure minute by minute! It can turn a sunny day cloudy, and get your juices flowing when you're calm. It's sort of the ultimate way to make sure that you and everyone around you are attached to the electrical grid of high tension every second. I think if I were to tell you the one sure way to jam the gears of everyone anywhere near you, it would be to embrace envy. In fact, if you have enough envy, you don't even need poison.

❧ ❧ ❧

9

Be a Perfectionist

In your life, everything and everyone has to be perfect. Don't be satisfied with yourself or anyone else unless what you do is absolutely impeccable. Don't just do it well enough to get by; torture yourself until it's perfect, and torture everyone around you, too. In fact, keep in your mind the powerful injunction that *everything* you do has to be perfect. And then you'll be so paralyzed with inaction that you won't do anything at all for fear that it won't turn out just right.

For example, your husband suggests that you learn how to garden so you can spruce up the outdoor area. Sure, it might not be a bad idea (although let's remember that only *you* truly have good ideas, not anyone else). But could your roses ever compare with those at the gardens at Versailles, or the White House? Probably not. Then why bother to even try? Or maybe you think you should write a letter of sympathy to someone who's lost a parent. Well, for one thing, the world revolves around *you*, not anyone else. But also, and this is very important, your note might not be as good as Shakespeare could have crafted it. So why do it at all?

This one is a jewel. Just tell yourself before you buy a computer that you simply have to get the best buy on the Internet—and watch, you won't end up purchasing anything at all. If you're going to get a new car, you have to get the best bargain anyone has ever gotten in the history of car buying—otherwise, you ain't plunking down that check. If you plan to write a paper, make sure it's going to be the best one since the Gettysburg Address. But you know it won't be that good, so why not just blow it off?

You get the picture, you genius, you! If you handle your life in just this way, you'll soon do nothing at all unless it's perfect, and since that might not turn out to be the case, well . . . next thing you know, you will simply, again, do zero.

❖ ❖ ❖

10

✻ ✻ ✻ ✻ ✻ ✻

Think Too Big

Set enormous, unattainable goals. Don't just be content to teach your son how to cast a fishing line on a sunny Sunday morning. Instead, seclude yourself and plan to create a company out of your garage that will be bigger than Microsoft. And then take a nap. Or have a drink.

Here's another: Instead of simply enjoying the afternoon breeze while you help your husband clear the leaves from the lawn, read in the financial magazines about people who have made billions selling T-shirts from the back of their car. Then make plans to be even bigger and richer than they are, and completely avoid enjoying the loveliness of the moment. Don't just do what's in front of you, like your work at the office or your shopping or your schoolwork. No, that's far too puny for you. You're a world beater, a conqueror. The small achievements and enjoyments of life are far too trivial for you. When you think about a task, make it so elaborate and complex that it never gets completed.

And this is closely connected to the next piece of guidance . . .

❦ ❦ ❦

11

Don't Enjoy the Simple Things in Life

Ignore life's little pleasures. Don't take pleasure in a child's smile. Don't enjoy a sunset. Don't take pleasure out of a simple but well-cooked meal. For you, things have to be elaborate, intricate, and incomprehensibly grand to make any sense. So just gloss over a friendly smile from a clerk or a pat on the back from a friend. Go for the big stuff. And if you can't get it, be miserable about the fact that the world has cheated its only deity . . . again.

12

❖ ❖ ❖ ❖ ❖ ❖

Fix Anyone and Everyone at Any Time

This is a big one, so take notes:

Form relationships with people who have lots of problems, and believe in your heart you can *change them*. Yes, this is perhaps the supreme piece of advice, so please don't forget it: *Believe in your heart that you can do the impossible—change and fix people.*

Marry the guy who can't keep a job and drinks too much every day and night. Then, tell him sharply that you want him to stay sober, get a good job, and keep it. Nag him and badger him and throw out his liquor, and cry when he goes to the bar. Pretty soon, you'll have him stone-cold sober. Yup, just for you, he'll do it, what no man has ever done before— stay sober as a result of a woman's nagging.

Or, move in with that woman who's broken every heart she's ever touched with her two-timing treachery. Tell her you expect her to be perfectly faithful, and for you, she'll stay on the straight and narrow. If you do catch her cheating, throw a fit and maybe throw away her favorite CDs—next thing you know, she'll purr like a kitten for you and only you.

Yes, you'll hear over and over again that people can't be changed, but that doesn't apply to you! You alone will be the very first human being ever to mold others to your desires. You can succeed where everyone else has failed. Human character may be totally immutable to most people—but not to you! And don't give up trying until you actually do make that change. It's just around the corner. That employee of yours who fakes being sick and sits around all day wasting company money? Sure, he'll change. The business partner who's a habitual liar and takes money from the cash drawer? Speak plainly but sharply, and you'll get the changes you want and deserve.

It used to be believed that years of brainwashing in a North Korean torture camp plus mind-altering drugs were the only techniques that could make a person change, and then not for long. But for you, it's all different.

People really do change—*but only for you.*

❦ ❦ ❦

13

❖ ❖ ❖ ❖ ❖ ❖

Treat the People who Are Good to You Badly

Who cares if they're good to you? They're your doormats—they exist solely for you to trample upon. They have nothing to say to you that's worth hearing. Basically, they're your servants. No, slaves. And they'll always be good to you because they sense that you're superior to them—and they're right. They know that you're a deity, and they're just insignificant pebbles on the bottom of the sea of life. Yes, you, of course, have the most intense and exquisite feelings. But no one else has emotions that need be taken into account. Just use them and abuse them and toss them away when you feel like it. Imagine how the Aztec gods treated their worshipers—causing them to be sacrificed and to have their hearts ripped out while still breathing. That's how you should treat the people who are good to you—although you can skip the drama.

If someone at your job is loyal to you, often stays late to get projects done, and then eventually needs your support to get a raise, tell him he's on his own. If you have a teacher who's patient with you and helps you learn something—as if you weren't born knowing it all!—don't thank her—just walk right past her on the last day of school without saying a word. If you have a friend who's listened to you when you continually bemoaned a lost love, don't even answer the phone when she calls to ask you for a favor.

Biting the hand that feeds you is one of the absolutely surest, most skillfully crafted weapons you possess. But then you already knew that, because (now I'm preaching to the choir!) you know *everything*.

Just in case you haven't committed it to memory, though, remember it now: You don't owe anyone a darned thing, and the people who are nice to you . . . well, they're just suckers and losers anyway. They're beaten-down curs that you can treat any way you please. And that old saw about treating people nicely and the Golden Rule and all that garbage . . . hey, those are just old wives' tales from a very old Book. Just forget about it. You know very well that you don't get to be rich and famous being considerate to others. It's *their* job to treat *you* well, and it's your absolute right to treat them like dirt.

❦ ❦ ❦

14

※ ※ ※ ※ ※ ※

Treat the People who Are Bad to You well

That's right. They'll soon change and start being really, really good to you. Maybe. But whether they do or not, let's be honest about this: Some weird urge in you tells you to knuckle under and treat the people who are bad to you *really* well. In some way you can't quite explain right now, the people who treat you like dirt will greatly enrich your life some-where down the road if you just treat them really nicely—preferably ignoring those who were good to you in the process.

The gal who two-timed you when you were madly in love with her? Buy her jewelry.

The agent who promised he'd get your deal done and then slept on the job? Forget about it. He'll be really useful to you someday, so give him a flat-screen color TV. Treating the real creeps in your life well gives you a lot of satisfaction and is actually a stress reliever. So keep doing it. It will pay off immensely, in the way that allowing yourself to be dumped on by bad people always does!

This is a mystery, but it's a good mystery: When you treat the people who show you contempt with nothing but respect . . . you'll find that you'll end up being a happy guy or doll. Someday.

❀ ❀ ❀

15

Hang Out with the Wrong Crowd

Associate with unlucky, unsuccessful people with revolting habits on a regular basis. Yes, no matter how bad your life seems, there will always be those who are drunker, have saved less money, have incurred more debts, have gotten into more trouble with the law, and are lonelier than you are. Make these people your pals. It will make you feel better to be around such sad sacks. You can feel superior all of the time. And their bad habits will never rub off on you, because you're perfect—even if the world at large doesn't know it yet. From now on, when you feel bad, you've got human support levels under you in the form of people who are worse off than you.

It's especially useful to hang around people who abuse drugs or alcohol or lie a lot or brag all of the time. And it's really a great idea to interact with individuals who are pretentious and boast without having a thing to brag about. And associating with people who never tell the truth will always pay off big. Plus, it's nice to be around people with no money, bad breath, dirty hair, and unkempt clothes. It's really top drawer if they reek of body odor as well.

These annoying habits will never ever stick to you, though. No, sir. No, ma'am. Instead, you'll become more and more successful just by associating with such a stellar crowd. You may have heard that others will be judged by their friends. *But not you.* No one can judge you because you're the supreme judge of humankind. Not only that, but you're so unique that no one will ever be in a position to adequately gauge your greatness, just as no one can look into a bright sun for more than a few moments . . .

So keep those human dregs around you, and see how much happier you'll be!

❀ ❀ ❀

16

❖ ❖ ❖ ❖ ❖ ❖

Make the People Around You Feel Small

That's it. Make 'em squirm. Belittle them on a regular basis, and brag as much as you can about your family, your job, your car, and the people you know. If your next-door neighbor has lost a bundle in the stock market, tell him how much money you just made with your own investments. If the poor guy looks crestfallen, tell him that you wouldn't have made the mistakes he's made in a million years. If the woman in the next cubicle just broke up with her boyfriend, tell her how long you've been happily married.

If your secretary tells you that her car keeps breaking down, make a point of reminding her that your car never has any problems and is always in great shape. Don't disguise the scorn you feel for her—how stupid could she have been to buy such a crummy car in the first place?!

You can accomplish all of this really skillfully, too. Stick the knife in when your colleague is really down and depressed. Do it especially when it has to do with money. This one can really hurt. Just run wild with your boasting. Brag as much as you can about everything in your life. (But again, concentrate on money, which can really turn the screws.) Some might think that this will make the people around you despise you. But you know better (and anyway, who cares, since you're a walking godhead and everyone else is just there to worship you). Acting in this manner may actually make everybody else really look up to you and even worship you. They want to be insulted and humiliated—maybe not by anyone else—but by *you*, sure! In fact, it's a privilege for them to have you lord it over them . . . and they'd better learn to like it!

❖ ❖ ❖

17

✿ ✿ ✿ ✿ ✿ ✿

Keep Score

Keep a running tally of life's injustices, and get really angry about every single one of them. Yes, we all know that the world isn't meant to be fair—except where *you're* concerned! (And in that case, it's supposed to be *more* than fair.) But again, don't even think about whether it's equitable for anyone else. Your justifiable anger over anything that's not perfect for *you* is all that counts.

Don't think about the undeniable fact that there are small children in cancer wards. What matters is that the waiter at your juice bar was rude to you. It's none of your concern that people are being sold into slavery in the Sudan right now—hey, the lettuce in your salad isn't crisp enough! And what about that guy who did so much better than you in school? He must have cheated. And how come your house didn't go up in value as much as your sister's? You've been robbed, my friend, and we both know it. Yes, it's a beautiful day, and you're feeling healthy, but what about the bum advice your stockbroker gave you last month? You wuz robbed! This is more than envy. This is about letting the universe know that you're owed a better deal. Get furious and hold on to that anger, as well as that feeling of being cheated. That will most assuredly help you get through your day really steamed, which is a lot more interesting than just feeling cool and collected.

When you feel as if you might be having a great day, recall some real or imagined slight that someone inflicted upon you. Remember when your friend insisted on sitting in the front seat of the car that time you were on a double date? Or think about a stock you bought that went up right after you sold it. Maybe you can recall someone who cut ahead of you in line at the airport ten years ago. And what about that old college friend who's ended up being so much more successful than you?

Let's get serious. There's nothing to be happy about when you start to carefully ponder every possible thing to be *miserable* about. Surprise!—you'll find that the list is almost endless. Just continue keeping score, and you'll find that you're always losing. And keep that anger burning red hot, churning up your stomach, preventing you from sleeping, and keeping you from appreciating the beauty around you. Anger is its own reward, and so is feeling perpetually cheated.

※ ※ ※

18

Use Drugs and Alcohol Freely

This is another huge one:

Tune in, turn on, and wreck your life. True, you may have heard that there's no human so powerful or lofty that drugs and alcohol can't bring that creature to the gutter. Yes, drug and alcohol abuse can wreck the lives of superstars and billionaires. Every entertainment magazine is full of stories of men and women who were on top of the world and were brought to their knees by poverty, insanity, and premature death by overuse of drugs and alcohol. Since you're a special genius, you know that the mental hospitals of this country are loaded with men and women who got there by being high and staying high. You've probably known family members who ruined their lives (and their family's lives as well) as a result of drug and alcohol addiction. Yes, drugs and alcohol used to excess are deadly poisons for most people.

But you're different. You can drink day after day and not get dependent on it. Truth is, you're funnier, sharper, better looking, and more confident with a little booze in you. It brings out your natural sophistication and wit. You get to be like one of those lively, charismatic characters you see in films, like James Bond—"shaken, not stirred," ha ha. Nah, alcohol is no problem for you. You've tried it and you like it, but you can quit any time. In fact, you've quit two dozen times. Sure, the sauce makes you argue with your spouse and neglect your kids. But you know what? If liquor was so bad, why would it be sold on every street corner? Why would you see people on TV every day merrily belting it down? And if a celebrity can handle it, you can, too, my mighty friend.

Now what about those drugs? The reefer, the weed, the Ecstasy, the pills? Well, what the heck were they invented for? I mean, life stinks when the world doesn't recognize your greatness, and it's really only bearable when you're high on something. You'll never become an addict like those other losers, and all of those warnings are just scare tactics for punks.

Look, half the doctors in America are high on prescription drugs right now. You know it for a fact. You read it somewhere. Or maybe someone told you at your office. And the drug companies make billions peddling the stuff—and they're big, respectable public corporations. So how bad can drugs be? I mean, if you can get a doctor to write a scrip for a drug that calms you down or gives you a little buzz, why can't you just forego that visit to the medical building? And why not just skip the whole medical establishment route and simply call your pal from college and buy a lid? Or a gram or two? It's not just that it makes you feel better. It's *cool*. The coolest people in films do it. The coolest kids at your school do it. Why shouldn't you do something that makes you feel good and is also distinctly hip?

That stuff about one drug leading to a stronger one doesn't apply to a man or woman with your willpower. You're far too strong to even consider getting dependent on marijuana and then needing something stronger like heroin to get through the day. True, you've found it pretty rocky sledding when you did try to get through a day without your drugs, but if it were really important, you could just chuck 'em any old time. Let's remember: You're the boss. The drugs work for you. You own them. They don't own you—and no matter what they've done to other people, drugs will never control *you*.

So, when you want to start feeling a little better, don't hesitate to take out the bottle or the pills. You deserve a break today—and every day. It's your God-given right to avoid ever feeling any emotion you don't want to feel. So if drugs and alcohol do it for you (and why shouldn't they?), hey, go for it!

❦ ❦ ❦

19

❖ ❖ ❖ ❖ ❖ ❖

Don't Save Any Money

Repeat after me: "I don't need no stinkin' savings!" Thrift? That's for fraidy cats and nerds. You're always going to have a great job or score big on the stock market or have "friends" you can take advantage of. Money will be like low-hanging fruit on trees all around you. There won't be any rainy days in *your* life. Money will just pour in by magic. Plus, in the remote event that your money flow slows down a bit, you have a special flexibility that no one else has. You can live just as well spending a little or a lot. Many people have problems adjusting to having less money to spend. But not you. You can live on a million dollars a year or on nothing flat. You're like a Buddhist holy man. You're far above the petty gravity of money. So, it doesn't matter if you have money saved. You are you, indestructible and defiant.

Plus, let's think about it for second. Savings are for people who don't know how to enjoy life in the moment. But *you* have a special sense of how to appreciate life. You like to spend money when you feel good—*and when you feel bad*—you dog, you. You know precisely how to use your cash when you want something and not hold back. The people who cheat themselves by not spending when they should be enjoying themselves? Losers! Something you will never be. You're a champagne-and-caviar kind of individual, and if others aren't, that's their problem.

I mean, it's not like you're ever going to get old and be retired and still need money to live on. You're not going to ever lose your job and have to go without sleep worrying about paying your mortgage. You won't ever need the down payment on a house. Far from it. No, it'll always be smooth sailing and a cloudless sky. The money will just keep pouring in.

Recessions and layoffs are words in someone else's vocabulary, not yours.

And if you do hit a rough patch, you can always scare up some loser who did save, and scrounge money from him. Why do you think the Almighty made savers and little insignificant people who squirrel away money? So that they can be around to lend (really, *give*) you money. True, you may have heard that "neither a lender nor a borrower" should you be. But that doesn't apply to you, friend. In fact, it's a privilege to lend to someone as great as you. Many people go through life just saving, saving, saving. *Boring!* And what good does it do them? It might as well be donkey dung. No, the only way it would do them any good is if they used it to get closer to a sweetheart like you. So do them a favor: Don't save, and let them have the chance to lend you money down the road.

You ask, "What if they won't lend me money when I'm in need?" Honey, that's not possible. Not for a doll like you. What if it rains bananas? Don't save, and you'll be fascinated by what happens if you need money suddenly. It won't just be your genial next-door neighbor or your ex-wife or your long-lost cousins who rush to help you out. No, far from it. It will be the "Big Boys": Credit card firms, auto loan companies, banks, insurance agencies—all of them will happily postpone your payments indefinitely if you just give them a handshake and a smile. No, of course they don't do that for just anyone. But for you, life without money will be a breeze. Friends, creditors— basically everyone in your life—has a secret wish to accommodate you when you're a little short in the bread drawer. Just spend and spend and let the money run out, and you'll be pleasantly surprised by how easy life is without any funds.

Money is like drugs and alcohol to you: You can do great with it or great without it. You're in charge.

❖ ❖ ❖

20

Ignore Your Family

Get rid of those balls and chains. This is contrary to what you may have heard from other folks, but it's true, nonetheless—at least for you! Family? They're just a burden on you anyway. Who needs 'em? Sure, they're there for you whenever you need companionship and support (as if a superhero like you needed such trivialities—ha!). That's right, when the rest of the world has forgotten you, they're there. So freaking what? You have to be a rolling stone, a freewheeling guy with no attachments, Jack Nicholson in *Easy Rider*. You have to be Marlon Brando in *The Wild One,* and Keanu Reeves in *The Matrix*. You have to be free to act out your dreams and fantasies. A family only slows you down.

Of course you want them around when they can do something for you, but when they need *you,* the hell with 'em. Responsibilities such as paying bills and helping to cook dinner? Forget it. When did James Bond have to pay utility bills or help with the algebra homework? No, that's not for a secret agent/playboy/rock star like you. You think Dirty Harry had stacks of bills to pay? Or spelling lists to help his kid with? No way. Look, you might condescend to be there when your son scores the winning goal. You'll show up if your daughter is elected homecoming queen, sure. But if they have problems, it'll do 'em good to work them out by themselves. That's how character gets built. Just ignore your kids when they need you, and see how big and strong they grow up to be. (And how happy and proud *you'll* be if you know in your heart that you ignored them when they were young.)

Yes, I know. When you ignore them, it's not always pretty. They may cry or look hurt, but that's just part of growing up. If they were as smart as you are (and who is?) the kids would know that you're doing them a huge favor by forcing them to make it on their own. I mean, teenagers are always whining that they want to be left alone. Well, here's their chance. You'll be off living it up and saving the universe and sleeping late. In the end, both you and the kids will be a lot better off.

Your parents? Screw 'em. They're boring, and what the heck did they ever do besides nag you? In fact, their behavior is usually outrageous, practically unforgivable. They tell you, mighty *you,* what to do. You! That's right. They tell you to eat right, to get enough sleep, to save your money, to be careful. Can you believe that? That's like telling a river how to flow or the stars how to shine.

Maybe they did some things for you when you were a child. Maybe they fed you and sheltered you and cleaned up your poop. Maybe they were patient with you when no one else would be. Maybe they were in your corner when you would have been alone. So what? That was what they were supposed to do. How many times do they have to get the message? They did their job, and now it's time to move on to bigger and better things.

And by the way, in the extremely unlikely event that anyone would say there's anything wrong with you, it's your parents who screwed you up. Let's not forget that. Those old folks who try to look so sweet and innocent and harmless? By every psychiatric theory, parents are to blame for everything. So if you're a bit selfish sometimes and don't always remember every single little detail of what you're "supposed" to do, whose fault is that? *Right-o—their* fault, and no one else's. So, forget 'em, I say. They're lucky that you don't report them to someone—even now when you're 30 or 40. And if you find yourself feeling lonely without them, just have a drink. Or buy something.

Your spouse keeps demanding your attention when you should be getting it all? And he/she expects you to actually do things around the house? I mean, what are wives and husbands for? To look good and be available for sex in the event you feel like having it, that's what! After that, they might as well be prison guards. If they're just gonna tell you what to do, who needs 'em? A mate should just be there when you want something, and then be still and silent the rest of the time—like a comfy chair. If wifey or hubby can't do that, just get 'em the hell out of your life.

Family is highly overrated. You'll do great without them. And really, they'll be better off, too. The world is such a warm, friendly place that it just makes sense for people to be out in it as individuals, not with anyone on their team—especially not if it means any real effort by you. Just ditch your family . . . but by all means, do expect them to be there for you if you need help on the spur of the moment!

❖ ❖ ❖

21

Know That the Rules of Reasonable, Decent Conduct Don't Apply to You

Rise above it all.

Let me give you a few examples—as if you needed them:

Income taxes: They're a major pain in the butt to figure out. You have to collect all kinds of documents, go through them, sort them, make notes, and then you often have to shell out some cash. Sometimes a lot of cash. Well, only idiots pay their full income taxes. (Don't you recall that fine example of a noble life, Leona Helmsley, saying that ". . . only little people pay taxes"? Learn from her, you big, lovable lug.) In fact, why bother to submit a return at all? It's a ton of work, and hey, there are hundreds of millions of other people filing their returns. What the heck does the IRS need one more for? The employees at the IRS are just ordinary working schmoes like you. Why burden them with extra paper?

And if and when you do file and do it wrong, don't worry. The IRS will never catch you. If they do, they'll just chuckle and tell you to please not do it again. Everyone knows that the IRS is good-natured and sweet and easy to get along with. Have you ever had an audit? Then you know very well what great people they are. They love a good laugh, especially at their own expense. They're just a bunch of bureaucrats who want to hang around the water cooler all day telling dirty jokes. Save them a little work, and save yourself a lot, and see how grateful the IRS folks are. (Again, if you do file, don't even think of paying what you actually owe. Just pay what you feel like. It's enough of a pain in the butt to pay anything at all as it is. You've got to leave *some* for yourself. Let the other poor slobs pick up the slack.)

Driving: Hey, pal, you own the road. Drive any old way you please. Only geeks go the speed limit. You're in a hurry. And besides, you were born knowing how to be a racecar driver. Those speed limits apply to little old ladies and wimps. You could drive 80 anywhere in any city or on any highway with your eyes closed—and sometimes I'll bet you do, you rascal!—and never have a problem. The least a true Indy-class driver like you can do is drive at any speed you find comfortable.

Buckle up your safety belts? Why? You're not going to crash, and hey, the belt makes your shoulder itch. Besides, you read somewhere that it's better not to wear your safety belt because you can get trapped in your car when you need to get out in an emergency—like to have a drink or buy something.

Signal when changing lanes? What for? That's someone else's problem, not yours. Tune up your car and get your brakes checked? You would if you had time, but you're busy. Let the other people on the road worry about *you*. You don't have the time right now to worry about *them*. Anyway, you're never going to have an accident. I mean, you've never even gotten a ticket, right?

Smoking: Hey, you're not a baby. You can do what you want. So what if there's a mountain of data that warns that smoking can kill you or give you cancer that eats away at your tongue and liver and lungs? Didn't you just see a WWII movie with John Wayne where all those guys were smoking? And weren't they as tough as old boots? Sure they were. Remember how The Duke kicked all that Nazi ass? Not only that, but in every gangster movie, those guys are smoking. So why can't you? And didn't you meet some guy who told you that his uncle smoked all his life and lived to be 88? Hey, George Burns smoked lots of cigars and lived to be 100! Plus, smoking makes you feel good. Just one drag, and that rich, lovely nicotine is all over your lungs and blood making you feel safe and secure. Take a deep puff and watch a third of the cigarette turn to ash that goes right to your immortal cardiopulmonary system. Enjoy yourself!

Planning for the future: No way. You're a happy-go-lucky guy or doll. You need to enjoy the moment. It takes too much brainpower to think beyond this very moment. It creates furrows in your forehead, so why the heck bother? Actually write down some plans and some numbers and try to live within them? Uh, I don't think so. I believe that spells "N-E-R-D," and that ain't you. Did you ever see James Dean making little budgets or plans on a sheet of yellow legal paper? Did you ever see Clint Eastwood doing it or Tom Cruise? What about Liz Taylor or Julia Roberts? Then why would *you* do it? Do you think that a living, breathing deity has to make dopey little plans? No, *you* control the future, so why should you have to worry about it? The future will be whatever you want it to be.

Home ownership: Buy a house so you won't be paying rent all of your life? That's too much hassle. It's a lot of work to fill out all of those mortgage forms. Plus, you have to shop around and pack up and move. But hey, maybe a good fairy will just magically move you to a house. Anyway, this all comes under the heading of worrying about the future, and that's a big no-no. You already know this, but . . . the future will take care of itself. You don't have to do a darned thing you don't want to do.

Being reliable: Return things you borrow? Why? They're *your* things now! Besides, who cares? There will always be another sucker to give you whatever you need. Return *money* you borrow? I don't think so! I mean, what on earth is the point of borrowing money if you have to pay it back? What good does that do you? You'd just be in the same position you were in before if every asset was also a liability. For royalty like you, there's really no such concept as "borrow." There's "give," as in "gimme"; and "take," as in "I'll take that." Those are the only options, and by God, we know who the taker is in this world. It's you, you, you. I want to emphasize this again. Why borrow if you just have to repay? No, don't even think about it.

Hygiene: Oh, here's a good one: Don't bother to keep yourself neat and clean. Of course you can't stand the smell of body odor and bad breath and stale cigarettes and whiskey on others. It's disgusting. But when it emanates from you, it smells like the finest French perfume. You have the right to expect others to be fresh as a daisy, but *you* don't have to be. That's not in your job description, any more than it's expected that babies or Greek gods would have to dress themselves and keep themselves spic and span. You can look any old way you want, and people will be happy to have you around, period.

Yup, when it comes to any of the above situations, you can do whatever the heck you feel like—but you get to complain and criticize every other person on earth for any old reason you want! And that's what rising above it all is all about!

※ ※ ※

22

Live As If Truth Is Relative— a Distant Relative

Don't tell the truth if you don't feel like it. The "truth" is just a way to hem you in, control you, and tie you up in knots when you have to "confess" to things that might seem a little embarrassing to you. The real truth, the one that matters, is whatever works for you and saves your behind. There's no objective truth except what's good for you, sister. And who cares if you get caught lying? That's someone else's problem. No one else can judge you. Only *you* can judge you. I think Charlie Manson once said that, didn't he?

Truth, like paying taxes, might be a factor for the little person, but it doesn't exist for you. Truth is a lovely thing for poets and philosophers to talk about, but it doesn't mean a thing to you if it gets in your way. I mean, think about it like this: Great nations often tell fibs in diplomatic situations. They say they won't attack and then they do. They say some dude wasn't a spy when he was. If nations can do that, why can't you? You're at least as important as any country that ever existed, aren't you?

And by the way, last time I looked, you weren't a prisoner in some damned Commie country. You don't have to confess to anything. You're allowed under the Constitution to lie all you want. Don't politicians do it? Don't business owners do it? Don't they do it in advertisements for hair-replacement products and stuff like that all of the time? Then why can't *you* do it? Why on earth, in a world where lying is commonplace, should you ever have to tell the truth? And so what if you betray people's trust? That's their problem. You aren't the freaking tooth fairy or whoever's in charge of the truth. You are you—a living, breathing deity—and the truth is just dirt under your gilded feet.

On the other hand, if telling the truth advances your cause, then everyone else has to be bound by it, too.

Maybe I can make this even more clear: All concepts and principles exist for you to either use or ignore, depending on whether they help you or not. If it doesn't help you, it's bogus, and if it does help you, it's great. It's that simple, because, hey, you're at the center of the universe, with all of creation revolving slowly around you.

❖ ❖ ❖

Remember That No One Else Counts

Always remember that relationships are worthless. Now, you may have heard a silly rumor that relationships are vital and that the most important book you'll ever own is your own Rolodex. And you may also have heard that you have to be good to people because you might need them someday.

This is nonsense. You know better. You can and must treat people any old way you want. You don't ever need to think about doing favors for others or being good to them so they'll remember you and be there to help you get a job or get your child into school. People will always want to do whatever you want them to do *at the exact moment* you want them to. No matter how you treat them, they'll be right at your beck and call. Ordinary people aren't even going to remember whether you helped them when they needed something. They won't hold a grudge if you treated them poorly. Far from it. No, instead, they'll very much want to assist you in any possible way. In fact, you can treat all of the people you know like dirt (or, like the lowly mortals they are) and they'll still want to help you at any time.

Let me give you an example. You have a desire to get a job in show business, and you happen to have a cousin who works in the entertainment industry. Well, don't bother showing him any kindness or courtesy. Borrow things and don't return them. Make fun of him. Bait him on his political and religious beliefs . . . because you know that even then, he'll be perfectly happy to do whatever he can for you!

Or suppose you have a relative who's a doctor. She could help you deal with that persistent cough you've had for about 15 years (gee, could smoking have anything to do with it?). Maybe she might even know a painless way to get you off tobacco. So, the thing to do is . . . don't remember her birthday. Don't lift a finger for her. Don't inquire about her children or her husband. Just treat them all like dirt . . . and they'll be ready to help you anyway. Remember how I told you that it's best to treat the people who are good to you badly and treat the people who are bad to you well? This is just another example.

Besides, why would a guy or gal like you ever need any kind of help anyway? Did Zeus need any help? Did the archangels of the Lord? No, and neither do you. You came from the womb perfect, without any need for human companionship or assistance. Relationships are just baggage, like family. And if you do need people at some time, they'll be ready to help just because you're you. That's more than enough reason. This may seem to be a bit similar to some other rules about mistreating other people, and maybe it is. But I need to reiterate it to remind you that you can't ever place too low a value on human relationships.

❖ ❖ ❖

24

Know That You Don't Owe Anyone a Thing

Hold this thought: Obligations are for suckers. The universe was made for your enjoyment, not for you to do anything for anyone else. Your boss wants something from you? Too bad. Why would that jerk think you owe him a thing just because he pays you a salary? What a freaking money-grubbing creep! You're owed that money just for being there or really, just for existing. You don't have to do a damned thing for it.

Your spouse expects you to be somewhere to help with a project? The heck with it. You have your own plans. (Remember, families are worthless.) You're not anyone's slave. You have a right to do whatever you feel like doing anytime you want. Why would anyone think that he or she owns you? Didn't I already explain how the 13th Amendment ended slavery? Well, just lay it out for whoever's asking: You have your own needs and plans and wishes. You don't owe anyone else a damned thing!

Some old biddy who was a pal of your mom's wants something from you? Maybe she's the same woman who got your mother a job to help her pay her way through college? Hey, is that ancient history or what? Who the heck cares? It was long ago and far away, and that's all there is to it. I mean, you have important things to do today—like that big football game you want to watch on TV. Just forget all about any sense of obligation to anyone.

This country? Someone actually expects you to be grateful for the soldiers who fought and died to keep this country free? Why? Fuggetabout it. You didn't know any of those people, did you? That all happened a long time before you were even born. They didn't know you. They didn't do it for you. They did it because they enjoyed freezing in France and getting their arms and legs blown off while they were starving. They did it because they had nothing better to do. They wanted to land on red sand in Iwo Jima and have a Japanese land mine blow them and their friends into little pieces. They were crazy. Besides, they got paid, didn't they? So why are they all over your case about it? It's their problem if they happened to get in the way of a bullet or a shell. It's over and done with anyway. You don't owe them nuttin'. The men and women fighting and dying in Afghanistan? Hey, that's a long ways away.

And the teachers who taught you in school? Weren't they just royal pains in the butt? They kept you from getting your much-needed sleep. You still despise them. Some of them gave you bad marks because you didn't turn in your homework—as if a creature of shining immortality like you ever had to do anything after school except hang out with your friends or watch TV. They failed you when you didn't know any answers on a test. Well, duh! Where did they get the idea that you had nothing better to do than study?

Teachers have no sense of duty or love of children. You know that, even if a lot of suckers don't. You're well aware that teachers are just in it for the big fat paycheck. They may fool the old folks, but they don't fool you, do they? No way are you going to show any respect for a bunch of losers who *teach* because they can't actually *do* anything.

And that's the bottom line: The world expects you to be grateful to a whole lot of people and institutions, and that's so darned wrong.

Everyone else should be grateful to *you!* I could go on about this, but a genius like you knows it the moment you read it: You don't owe anyone else a thing.

❀ ❀ ❀

25

Gamble with Money

Roll dem bones! Think about it logically. You already know you're the luckiest person who ever walked the earth. So why not make it official and actually lay down some bucks to prove just how lucky you are? True, Las Vegas and Atlantic City exist mostly because the gambler usually loses. But you know very well that the ordinary rules of life don't apply to you. The little ordinary gambler or even the high roller is a loser if only for one huge reason: He's not you! You're perfect! How could the heavens allow someone as impeccable as you to lose at anything? Maybe you might lose for a few minutes or hours or even years.

But over long periods of time, you'll surely be a huge winner at cards or races or sports. I mean, you're the winner of winners already, right? So why not make some big money at it?

And let's make this très simple, messieurs et madames: It's a fact that other people get their lives ruined by gambling and wind up impoverishing their families and themselves. Not only that, but it's quite rare to find someone who's been a long-term winner in gambling. But what difference does that make to *you?* You're not susceptible to what happens to the usual clod. You'll win and become fabulously rich. You're the one and only gambler in human history who will, at the end of the day, wind up in the black.

And, in fact, this amazing talent of yours is going to pull you through to glorious victory even when your friends are stumbling and suffering terribly in their puny efforts at little things such as work and saving. You'll watch them sweat and toil, but it won't matter a bit to you, because you're above the fray, tossing out chips that bring you mountains of moolah.

And don't confine your gambling to the roulette wheel or the craps table. No, no, no.

Gamble with speculative stocks. Gamble with commodities futures. Gamble with incredibly complex options you don't understand. They were invented so that very lucky men and women like you could make some real dough. Plunge right in! Plunk down your money and get ready for a ride to the moon!

(Hey! Don't forget to wager on sporting events, especially those you don't know much about. Your intuition is so acute that just *hearing* the names of the teams is enough to make you a winnah!)

So go ahead. Gamble. Live it up. And don't stop gambling just because you lose the first dozen or thousand times. Keep it up, friend. And be prepared for the glorious life that awaits you.

※ ※ ※

Make It Clear: Pets Are for Losers

Always keep in mind that pets are a pain in the ass. Now, you may have heard that a sweet little cat can keep you company and cheer you up in the worst of times. Or, that a big, warm, furry doggy can help you feel safe and peaceful when you have a string of terrible days. You may have friends (if you *have* any friends) who have told you that they owe their lives to dogs and cats who have kept them going when all else seemed lost. And you've probably heard that old chestnut about a dog being man's (and woman's) best friend.

Maybe so . . . for the weak and the meek. But you never have bad days. And you never feel weak or alone. You're all-powerful all the time. In the meantime, that darned dog or cat has to be fed, and you have to clean up the animal poopie! This is insane. Men and women at your level don't do such things, period. You do what you feel like doing, and that means that you don't clean up after anyone. (You don't even clean up after yourself, by the way, so why the heck would you clean up after a creature who can't help pay the mortgage or even read a book? Not that you read much anyway . . .)

Plus, dogs are always sniffing around and getting too close to you. The Roman emperors forbade anyone to touch them, except at their command. Similarly, any furry creature who would dare to touch *you* should be reviled. And dogs and cats need care. I've said it before and I'll say it again: You're not in the business of giving care. You're in the business of being worshiped without any reciprocal obligation.

So, let the weaklings have pets. You don't need the stinkin' hassle.

❖ ❖ ❖

27

Don't Clean
Up After Yourself

Throw away the apron. I know I've mentioned it before, but it's worth repeating: *You're a perfect being whom others are supposed to clean up after.* Just leave your dirty dishes and pots and pans lying around the house. Someone will clean it all up, even if you live alone. Leave your dirty clothes on the floor. That's not your job. You aren't a day worker in a plantation house. You have things to do, worlds to conquer. Look, you've seen *Star Wars*. Did Luke Skywalker or Han Solo go around doing laundry and folding clothes after ironing? Did either one of them clean the floors after Chewbacca had an accident? Now it's true that in *Gone with the Wind,* Scarlett did lower herself to do some cleaning. But that was only meant to show you how bad things had gotten. When things got better, she had servants to do the dirty work for her.

So freaking what if people complain that you're a slob? You don't live to please others (and there's another gem of truth for you!). You live to please *yourself,* plain and simple. (And other people live to please you!) So, get down and boogie, and let somebody else clean it all up. And if it gets too awful where you live because it's starting to look and smell like a pigsty, just move somewhere else (but make sure you leave your place a complete mess for the next tenant).

This also applies to emotional and financial messes. So what if you promised to love a man and he gave up his job and moved across the country to be near you? If you get tired of him, just cut him off without even a phone call. So what if you encouraged your partner to borrow money to start a business you were going to work with him on? If you changed your mind, that's his problem. You don't have to clean up the messes you've made. That's for the little people.

Your job in life is to please yourself moment by moment. I don't think that includes going around with a mop or a dustpan, whether real or figurative. Make any mess you want, and then go merrily on your way. It's your right.

❦ ❦ ❦

28

Have No Respect for Age or Experience

Respect gray hair? Why should you? You were born knowing everything. And you were especially born knowing that respect for elders is a waste of time. This goes back to the concept that the best way to do anything is *your* way. Tradition? That's nonsense. Skill based on years of practice? That's also poppycock. You happen to know more about everything than anyone else ever has or ever will. There's no such thing as hard work or industriousness that allows a man or woman to acquire a skill. Artisanship? Skilled craftsmanship that can create beauty? Big freaking deal. You know that you could do it better if you only bothered to try, and if you don't try, then that's because it's not worth doing in the first place.

Gray hairs and calluses mean nothing to you. With your childlike youth (no matter your age), you can do better at anything than anyone else can or ever will. So scoff at age and experience. No one's got anything to teach you. You might hear that you shouldn't honk at an old geezer because maybe when he was young he risked his life for our country. Or maybe you shouldn't blow some old biddy off the sidewalk because she's devoted her whole life to caring for others. What's the difference? This world isn't about anyone else but you and what's easiest for you. If respect for others older than you are gets in your way, the heck with it. Plus, old people are often really weak and timid, and you can and should push them around just because you can.

Okay. Enough said. Just don't fall for that stupid trap of respecting age. What good will it do you? And, of course, you'll never get old yourself, so you don't need to worry about karma. You know what karma really is, anyway? It's whatever you want or need it to be for *you*.

❀ ❀ ❀

29

Show Everyone Around You That You're Holier Than Thou

Don't hide the halo. When anyone in your path does something you don't like, cite some passages from the Bible that make it clear that the other person is evil or a fool. When you're criticized (imagine!), quote some prayer or line from Scripture that compares your martyrdom with that of a famous saint. When you're served a dish of some kind at your friends' home, bring up some moral objection to eating it. This accomplishes the dual function of making your hosts feel bad for having wasted their time, and also making them feel as if they're spiritually deficient. This double whammy guarantees that you'll be considered superior to everyone in your world. So what if they resent you for making them feel lowly? Don't the great prophets and saviors always end up being persecuted? Is that not by itself a clear sign of your elevated position?

If you're in a house of worship, pray louder than everyone else. If the prayer is in a foreign language, make sure you speak up really loudly so other people will know you're proficient in Latin or Hebrew or whatever. If some political issue arises in conversation, such as waging war on terrorists, stop the conversation cold by saying that you're too pious and holy to even think about wars where people get hurt or killed. If anyone near you is discussing the stock market and you don't feel for the moment like bragging about your investment prowess, simply say that you don't feel like talking about "sordid money matters."

And if some fool whom you borrowed money from asks for it back, perhaps you can look at him pityingly and say, "'Tis better to give than receive." And maybe add a few lines about how sorry you are that this person is such a money-obsessed Philistine. Then sigh and say you're really too busy thinking about the Bible to have to be concerned with repaying a few trivial earthly obligations right now. Then look heavenward and mention "usury."

This, by the way, is a simply great way to ruin a marriage. Just act as if, overnight, you've become morally superior to your spouse, and see how it makes him or her love you all the more.

The world needs to know that you're a holy being, above this earthly vale, and this might as well start at home. This especially applies to young people. You'll really make a big start toward the grandeur that's your due if you present yourself as being "above" your elders. Begin by simply saying that you won't eat your mother's cooking because she's murdered animals to make it. Watch her face fall and the color rise to her face. Then tell your father that, whatever he does, there's blood on his money. And remind all of the people in the neighborhood that they're killers and imperialists and you're better than they are, or simply imply it by your disdainful facial expressions.

Yes. You can *feel* the holiness surging through you, can't you? Enjoy it.

This works almost unimaginably well for people you've known for the better part of your life. Try waking up one morning as your husband is making you sausage and say to him, "I don't eat the flesh of living creatures, and neither would you if you had any decency."

Or, when your wife starts getting dressed to go out to work, ask her if she realizes that the lipstick she's wearing was tested on poor innocent rabbits who were tortured to death so that she could look nice! Or, if your next-door neighbors' son has just joined the military, tell them how nice it must be to have a child who's in training to kill innocent people overseas.

It sure does ring people's bells to be called names and to have you lord it over them with your self-important, holier-than-thou attitude. Try it for a while, and see how much the little people love and worship you, their new god or goddess. It should really bring a smile to your face.

❖ ❖ ❖

30

Fight the Good Fight ...
Over Everything

Anything is worth fighting over. You have the blood of the Vikings or the Zulu or the Hebrew warriors or the Cherokee coursing through your veins. You're a killer. You're a man or woman who will brave anything to achieve the final victory. And no detail escapes your vision of triumph. That's why it's worth starting a fight over every little thing. Did the waiter bring the meat imperfectly broiled? Don't just send it back. Scream at him—and the maître d', too. Did your spouse get your shirts done with light starch instead of full starch? *This means war!* Berate the mate, and sue the cleaners—and the sooner the better. Did some jerk cut you off at the last light? Don't just mutter under your breath. Jump out of your car with a baseball bat and start swinging. Let a real brawl ensue.

Losers and wimps may try to tell you, "Hey, that's not worth fighting over." Well, maybe not for them—the good-for-nothin' weaklings! But you're strong and tough, and you always win. Plus, your majesty is of such grandeur that even the slightest affront to it is worth a fight. Many a geek and a nerd would say that if someone says 99 kind things about you but has one word of caution, you should ignore the latter. *No way*! You demand satisfaction. Out come the dueling pistols. Life and death hinge upon getting your way down to the last detail.

And please don't let long ties of blood or friendship stand in your way. If you've been insulted—no matter how trivially—you must fight over it, and fight to the death. Did your lover tell you she thinks of you "often during the day"? That's not good enough by a long shot. She should be thinking of you every second. Blast her for that! Did your boss tell you that you did a *pretty* good job on your assignment? What the hell does that mean? *"Pretty good"?* That ain't good enough. How dare he!

Always be on the highest alert for things to get your goat and irritate you, and you shall surely find them and fight the good fight. Stay in attack mode, and always be on the ready.

And don't count the cost, for heaven's sake. Do not, for example, ask yourself whether it's worth losing your job over a real or imagined slight. Just go ahead and spin out of control. So what if you lose your job? You'll get another. Is it worth losing your lover or a spouse's affections over an offhand remark? Of course it is. Nothing's going to get past you—no, sir.

Choose your battles? Heck, no. Why choose when you can fight *all* of them!

◎ ◎ ◎

Do It Your Way

You can do it in your special, unique way, no matter how anyone else does it. Just think of that old crooner, Frank Sinatra. He did it his way. So can you. There may be certain laughably obsolete, stolid, and boring conventions about the way you work your way up in a business or don't take on airs when you first join a company or move into a neighborhood. Ha! That's for other people. You just do it every and any old way that comes into your little head. You don't have to adjust to the rest of the world—the rest of the world has to adjust to *you*.

Is it really that complex? I mean, suppose you live out in Hollywood like yours truly. There's an audition for an acting role you really want, and you're called in. Well, don't get there on time. Arrive when you feel like it. And don't be respectful toward the people who are auditioning you. They're lucky you cared to show your face at a gathering of nobodies. And by all means, don't look neat and clean. Just wear some old, baggy warm-up clothes and let your stringy, oily hair hang down in your face. It wouldn't hurt if you walked in with a cigarette dangling from your mouth, too. That would be cool.

If you're in school and you want to do well in a class, don't pay any attention to what the teacher says. Don't even bother to read the homework assignments. Just do whatever you feel like doing and then get really huffy if your teacher cops an attitude about your work.

Looking for a mate? Treat any guy or doll who comes along like dirt. Just talk about yourself and never ask about them.

And on the job, laugh at your boss and make fun of her behind her back and also right in her face. Bosses like to be mocked by their employees. And anyway, who the heck cares what your boss thinks? Just do it your way, without regret or sorrow.

The whole world is watching to make sure you do it your way and no other. They never expected you to follow their routine. Humankind has been waiting for thousands of years for that one guy or doll who wouldn't knuckle under—and you're the Messiah of Doing Your Own Thing. All hail!

❀ ❀ ❀

32

Think the Worst of Everyone

Always expect the worst of everyone. Why not? You know that in their hearts, they're all rats and creeps who just can't wait to stick it to you. They're all snakes in the grass hoping against hope for a chance to do you in or sneak up behind your back and harm you in some way. Why give them the chance? Strike first by expecting that they'll do you wrong. Then you can easily justify being suspicious and sarcastic and nasty and untrusting. Plus, you can insult them and lie to them and make sure that you bring out the behavior that was just waiting for a chance to get out anyway.

Some fools say that if you expect the best from people, you'll often get it. What a silly, infantile lie. In fact, you should always assume that people have the worst possible motives, never tell the truth, and will act dishonestly if given half a chance. So, be smart about it. *Don't give them half a chance.* Be on guard, suspicious, and defensive right off the bat. Then they can't slip any tricks by you like pretending to be fairminded or generous or trustworthy. People sometimes do that for years on end, just to lull you into a false sense of security. Don't let it happen to you. Put a halt to any good behavior others might show you by erecting a wall between you and them, and then pour boiling oil on the invaders of your great kingdom, whoever they may be.

◈ ◈ ◈

33

◈ ◈ ◈ ◈ ◈ ◈

Live Above Your Means

Live it up. Now, this is probably simpler than you realize—it's even more basic than the rule about not saving any money. *You can afford anything you want just because you want it.* If you see it in a magazine, you deserve it. If you have a friend who has a car, then you deserve to have that automobile as well. If someone you know just went to Hawaii, you need to go there, too. The fact that you earn X entitles you to spend 150 percent of X. The fact that you have nothing in the bank (and why the heck should you?) cannot and *must not* stop you from buying anything you want. What are credit cards for? What's zero down payment for? It's for you, you, you to enjoy anything you want.

And please don't worry if you don't have the money to pay your bills. Just apply for a new credit card and transfer the balance to *that* card. Or borrow it from someone (but remember, don't pay it back), 'cause if you want to live in a certain lofty manner, there's no reason on earth why you shouldn't do so. Get hip to yourself. You deserve it all—and just because you have no clear way to pay for it, that's meaningless. Buy it anyway.

You are The Chosen One, and I guess I just have to keep telling you that, because you're so darned modest. The Chosen One will always be able to make money appear at the last moment, like the miracle of the loaves and the fishes. Miracles do happen where money is concerned. You can count on that. It's much more real than arithmetic or numbers on a credit card bill.

So go ahead. Live it up, and worry about tomorrow . . . tomorrow. Bottom line: Spend all you want—but don't save anything or you'll ruin the whole effect. It all adds up to a delicious sense of freedom.

❧ ❧ ❧

34

Be a Smart-Ass

You have to get in the last word, and the world needs your wisecracks. And don't let some sugary smooth talker keep you from doling out venom along with your wit. If some kindly fool utters a sweet comment to you, come right back at him with a smart-ass retort that will leave him gasping for breath. If he tells you your suit is nice, tell him he needs a new one. If he tells you your hair looks pretty, say, "I wish I could say the same for you," and then ask him when the last time was he saw a barber. If someone tells you she admires your car, tell her you hope she doesn't steal it. Add that if you had a car like hers, you'd be jealous, too.

While you're at it, make a joke out of everything. The world wants to hear you mock it from head to toe. If someone tells you that he's proud to be an American, remind him about slavery and ask him if he's proud of that, too. This performs the dual function of putting the guy in his place, showing how very clever you are, and also pointing out that you're holier than he could ever hope to be.

If a relative has put up some lovely religious statuary in her front yard, make some sarcastic remark about buying it at a thrift shop, and then ask in hushed tones if she realizes that she's being "anti" your religion by displaying it. This actually gets you a sort of hat trick: contempt, cutting off relationships, *and* showing what a wise guy you are.

There's a saying that the man who's a hero is the man who swallows a wisecrack. No. Not true. For everyone else, maybe, but not for you. The world needs to listen to your sneers and jeers—immediately and often. Other people should keep their traps shut—especially when they're around *you,* but you should feel completely comfortable humiliating and deriding everyone in your sphere.

❖ ❖ ❖

35

Whenever Possible, Say "I Told You So"

Pour salt on those wounds. If something bad happens to someone you know, don't sympathize. Don't identify. Don't share the pain. Instead, simply say, "I told you so," and explain how you would never have been duped into whatever evil befell the other person. The world needs to know that whatever they did wrong—however innocently or unavoidably—*you* wouldn't have done it, and you know better. It might smart a bit for others to hear it, but they need to know that there is a superior being among them who doesn't make the kind of mistakes they do. It does them good to know this. People will respect you and fear you more if you make them feel really bad about who they are. And saying "I told you so" is the perfect way to accomplish that feat.

❦ ❦ ❦

(I bet you thought you couldn't ruin
your life in just 35 simple steps, right?
Well, I told you so.
Just <u>kidding!</u>)

❦ ❦ ❦   ❦ ❦ ❦

AFTERWORD

Well, you're almost there. If you've been reading carefully, and if you've been thinking of ways to put all of these steps into action, you're well on your way to making the one and only life you have . . . ruinous. But there are just a few other little thoughts (and one big one) that make the scheme of self-destruction complete. First, in every situation, ask yourself, "Am I considering other people's welfare? Am I taking into account their points of view?" If you're doing either, you're probably not going to ruin your life quickly enough. You should also ask, "Am I acting like a big baby, or am I acting like a grown-up here?" If you're acting at all like an adult, you're also not doing yourself in well enough.

The key in every case is to be obsessed, self-ish, and immature. When you find yourself acting with kindness, generosity, prudence, or common sense, you're probably way off base and might even be wandering into the rules for making your life a success. That would be a grave error.

Now, let's be fair. It's entirely possible that you might accidentally show some selflessness or care in some situations, but not if you're always on guard. You might actually be empathetic if you don't remember to get down into a good defensive posture of mistrust right away. So, be lazy and rude and a spendthrift all at once by doing something like using money you should be putting aside for education for drinks and drugs—thereby jeopardizing your future, the lives of those around you, and society as a whole.

Finally, and most important: Don't believe in God. Or, to put it more precisely, believe and know in your heart that there *is* a God—and you are the One. This is really key to every other part of this little guidebook. Believe that you are the most important One, that everything you do is what counts, that no traditions or laws man-made or natural apply to you, and that neither mathematics nor the laws of physics nor medicine apply to you. And sure as shootin', you'll find yourself ruined. Believe that you control all of human destiny. Believe that you can determine the results of everything that happens on this earth. Believe that the whole world is one giant movie and you're the director. And, know that you're the boss, the puppet master, controlling every single aspect of everyone's life: chief critic, dictator, censor, and of course, beneficiary and inheritor of everyone else's labor. You're a pagan god of sorts, with no responsibility to anyone in return. You're not the god of love or compassion. You're the god who lolls about eating grapes someone else has peeled, deriving your pleasure from everyone else's sacrifice and owing nothing in return.

Then, and only then, will you truly understand who you are. And then—God help you.

❀ ❀ ❀   ❀ ❀ ❀

ABOUT THE AUTHOR

Ben Stein has had an amazingly diverse career, to which he is adding to up to the present day. To start with, he is the Emmy-winning host of the multi-Emmy Award–winning (seven, since it first aired in 1997) game show, *Win Ben Stein's Money,* on Comedy Central.

Stein is a native of Washington, D.C., and grew up in Silver Spring, Maryland, where he attended school with future notables Sylvester Stallone, Carl Bernstein, Goldie Hawn, and Connie Chung (none of whom have read this book). Stein's father was the well-known economist and public policy commentator and wit, Herbert Stein.

Stein is a graduate of Columbia University's undergraduate college, where he earned a B.A.

in 1966, with honors in economics. In those years, he was active in the civil rights movement, working in many locales to enfranchise African-Americans as voters and to secure equal rights for them under law. After college, he worked for a year as an economist with the Department of Commerce, and then graduated from Yale Law School in 1970 as valedictorian of his class (by election of his classmates). He has served as a poverty lawyer; a trial lawyer in false and deceptive advertising cases; and as a teacher educating students about the political and social content of film and TV at American University in Washington, D.C., the University of California at Santa Cruz, and at Pepperdine Law School, where he also taught securities law for five years.

In 1973, Stein became a speechwriter for Richard Nixon at the White House and then continued that work for Gerald Ford when he became President. Stein became a columnist for the *Wall Street Journal* in 1974. In 1976, he moved to Hollywood, where he became a screenwriter, TV writer, novelist, and syndicated columnist. He worked for Norman Lear's Tandem/TAT production company, where he helped to create the cult hit *Fernwood 2Night*.

He is the author of 17 books, including the acclaimed diary of his first year in Hollywood, *DREEMZ,* the analysis of the political attitudes of Hollywood; *The View from Sunset Boulevard,* the tale of drug addiction and ambition in Los Angeles; and *'Ludes,* on which the movie *The Boost* was based. He has also written extensively about personal and financial self-help issues in the classic, *Bunkhouse Logic;* and a guide to economic success over a lifetime, *Financial Passages.* Most recently, Stein has authored a book about the trials and triumphs of being a father of a young son. The book is called *Tommy and Me.*

Stein is the writer of the outline for the ABC miniseries *Amerika,* and is also the author of the outline and the producer of the esteemed television movie *Murder in Mississippi,* about the martyred civil rights workers Goodman, Chaney, and Schwerner.

Stein has also written extensively about financial fraud and ethical duties in finance—mostly for *Barron's,* but also in a book about the Milken/Drexel fraud, *A License to Steal;* for a financial Website called "TheStreet.com; for *New York* magazine; and for the *New York Times Magazine,* among other publications.

In 1986, Stein became an "actor," when he played a teacher with a monotonous tone of voice in the classic comedy hit *Ferris Bueller's Day Off*. He was a recurring character, also playing a teacher, in *The Wonder Years* for three years, and has appeared in about 30 movies and TV series.

Stein lives in Beverly Hills, California, with his wife, Alexandra; his son, Thomas; and many dogs and cats. He is very active in fundraising for animal rights and children's rights charities in Los Angeles and throughout the country.

※ ※ ※　※ ※ ※

❀ ❀ ❀

We hope you enjoyed this Hay House book.
If you would like to receive a free catalog
featuring additional Hay House books and
products, or if you would like information
about the Hay Foundation, please contact:

Hay House, Inc.
P.O. Box 5100
Carlsbad, CA 92018-5100

(760) 431-7695 or **(800) 654-5126**
(760) 431-6948 (fax) or **(800) 650-5115 (fax)**
www.hayhouse.com

❀ ❀ ❀

Published and distributed in Australia by:
Hay House Australia Pty Ltd, P.O. Box 515,
Brighton-Le-Sands, NSW 2216 • *phone:*
1800 023 516 • *e-mail:* info@hayhouse.com.au

Distributed in the United Kingdom by:
Airlift, 8 The Arena, Mollison Ave., Enfield,
Middlesex, United Kingdom EN3 7NL

Distributed in Canada by:
Raincoast, 9050 Shaughnessy St.,
Vancouver, B.C., Canada V6P 6E5

❀ ❀ ❀